salmonpoetry

for Margaret

Acknowledgments

Acknowledgements are due to the editors of the following publications where many of these poems, or versions of them, have appeared: *Ambit, Cork Literary Review, Crannóg, Cúirt, Cyphers, Limerick Broadsheet, Orbis, Southword, The Irish Times, The Moth, THE SHOp, The Stony Thursday Book* and *The Warwick Review*.

CONTENTS

FARING

Here I am, still chugging
along these signposted roads:

trying to steer clear
of potholes and cul-de-sacs;

measuring my passage
through the rear-view mirror.

WORDS

I who as a child would fondle
murmur and *redolent* like toys;

who'd tiptoe through *omniscient*
or nestle in *oblivious*,

now find myself being lured into
another would-be poem,

its temptings, its untried openings:
wondering if *brood* is more resonant

than *ruminate*, or *Assisi*
less efficient than *Treblinka*.

BEATS

These fingers which register
word-spurts, which mark the rhythms,

press into your yielding flesh
like harbingers of love...

A life distilled to quickenings –
instinctive, mysterious –

across bare sheets towards
consummation, dreams

of trace and signature.

YIELD

Each working week, the tailbacks lengthen:
another amber turning red!
Our lives succumbing to mould and must;
    attrition, itchy needs...

Yet, when moments – a leaf-swirling
autumn evening; a bird's *ick-ick*;
or roads perilous with ice
    and snow – jolt me back,

it's all as vivid as shutter-snap.
A sanctuary lamp, its wavering flame.
A black ball poised on the pocket's lip.
    Your radiating name.

JOURNEYS

And what if I, too, could have set out,
desiring no more than smoother roads,
    the old ways made obsolete;
with warnings of dangerous bends;
with junctions, exits clearly shown?
    And so on to the end,

oblivious of other signs...
Never to miss sudden birdlift,
    a canopy of greens;
nor bear a fraying drift of midges;
nor feel beneath trim post-and-rail
    the ghostly reach of hedges?

BIRDSTRAINS

Again, those strains, as if
heralding the first spring —

and not these forbearing waters,
these buddings in helpless green;

not these bedded seeds set
for darker earth, darker yield...

Their notes so sticking in my throat
that I'd spurn all I have known,

if only it were as simple
as silencing them,

as killing two with the one stone.

GANNETS, DIVING

No turbulent brooding,
no fumbling for words...
Only an innate sense

of weather-shifts, sea-ripplings;
a fathoming of depths.
And the perfected descent:

those great wings folding
just a split second before
heads break the surface;

arrowing into
this elemental,
consummating catch.

POLAR

Drawn from old pub bubblings
to a TV programme
about polar bears

stranded on ice floes
or padding across
shrinking wilderness,

I saw as much
as anything else
the grand immutables

of my childhood drifting
past: surpliced acolytes;
unmolested whitethorn;

the tales of Shackleton,
Amundsen and Scott
sledding into legend...

Until someone
pressed a button
on the remote control.

SO MUCH

So much depends, too,

on ripples, aftermaths;
and how we read the signs.

What strains, what history
do these voices bear?

What dreams, what residues?
Or look farther out:

How is the canary
emerging from the mine?

Could a flutter
through the rainforest

create tremors
in the Himalayas?

KINDLING

Is it something that happens
between the first, elevating
drink, and closing time –

Wistful talk: the firefly gleam
of lost bearings,
fugitive offerings.

Or rambling soliloquies
on thistly pastures,
unbedded women.

Or tongues released in awe,
raising shrines to epic
matches, Derby winners –

which impels me homewards
to compose this reeling
that ripples through my depths?..

Jottings – stunted, brittle –
hoarded like kindling,
waiting for a spark.

RUTS

It would have been
just the usual night
in the local snug —

ruminative drinks,
neighbourly exchanges:
weather, matches, gossip —

were I not drawn
into an unheeded
TV documentary

about Salgaa,
a makeshift village
in the African bush,

where truckers would come, lured
by the prospect of cheap sex
in bars neon-flashing

Good Times, Shangri-la,
as big wheels turned the raw
streets into oozy mud...

And, homing, I couldn't erase
the spectre of those hovels
where AIDS-stricken girls,

their bones pushing against
papery, rash-marked skin,
were slipping beyond

the grasp of history;
beyond the clocks ticking
towards another nightfall,

and the trucks hurtling in.

RAPT

One night, near closing time,
seemingly out of nowhere,
Jody's boozy anecdote:

how a psychotic,
convulsed by menses,
would cast off her clothes

to go flouncing, babbling
through the asylum ward,
alarming staff and inmates...

But, afterwards, I worried
if, by my silence,
I had been complicit

in the sniggering
when he'd tried to mimic
those distressed imaginings,

and the nurses' words
and rhythms reining her in
towards equilibrium.

FERMENT

The revelations shocking us
into lives hardly articulate...
The still unravelling drama of abuse:
sandal-squeak at midnight; his fag-stained breath;
that unspeakable release.

To have lived for years like this,
each new day the spectre of yesterday.
Crumbling, shell-like, in a lover's embrace.
Numbing pain and shame with drink. Hatching,
hatching. Waiting for grace or ease.

To have lived for years like this,
never quite able to say it out...
Just sporadic splutterings, oblique tirades.
A spasm of fists flailing at shadows.
Wounds reopening. Splintered glass.

INTERIORS, WITH EMIGRANT IRISH

Camden, Kilburn, Cricklewood...
Once, many pubs; now, few:
a mouth of gapped teeth.

Evenings, I shuffle here,
and sit in drifting smoke,
amid froth-ringed glasses;

listening to men bursting
into drunken singing:
Far away from the land

of the shamrock and heather,
in search of a living
as exiles we roam.

While the notes rise and fall,
I start unravelling,
all my ties are shaken...

Closing time. Darkening
interiors. The old cry:
Have ye no homes to go to?

Outside, shops shut. Shuttered.
Rumbling, fuming traffic.
Round corners, wind pouncing.

Turning the key, I grope
for the bare mattress, the last
uplifting, numbing swig.

*

So what have I become?
Look at this place. No heat.
No water. Shadows, dust.

My bed, that sagging couch.
One bare, broken window.
Rows of empty beer cans.

Oh, I've had time enough
to mull over the *ifs*
and *buts*. Yet it's too late

to seek shape or outlet
for my downward drift.
And what is left to me?

Memories as worn as
this lino, persistent
as the rats scratching

in the dark...Going back
down the streets of Camden,
Kilburn and Cricklewood.

Recalling home. Sowing.
June meadows. The bells of
Angelus. Blighted spuds.

*

So there we are, fresh
off the boat from Ireland
in our Sunday-best: suit,

tie, shirt spotlessly white,
full heads of hair oiled back,
our shoes a sober black;

mumbling the names – Camden,
Kilburn and Cricklewood –
as if in litany...

After a day shovelling,
digging, hod-carrying,
to step out of the van,

hungry, tired, maybe wet;
and straight into the pub.
A fire, familiar

accents and flows of booze,
eyes brightening with laughter.
The rows of gleaming teeth.

To set out again
for the dancehall's throb and hum.
Neon lights flashing; beckoning

towards a dream-haze of girls.
Life pulsing through us, without
shadow or hangover.

GLEAM

i.m. Alex Higgins

Even when he'd shrunken
to a waifish figure,
hustling for a pittance –

his shots wobbling in jaws,
his attempted snookers
no longer surely judged –

the glories of his prime
lurked in memory's hold:
fugitive, stowaway…

There, in the arena's
altar hush. Eyes defiant,
vodka-lit, he swaggers

towards the baize, impatient
to ram in the balls.
Disdaining caution,

he deploys spin and screw
and stun to keep a wavering
break alive: the testing brown;

a sweet cut on the blue;
that awkward pink rolled down
the table's length. Leaving

the final sunken black;
his edgy gleam; the white
still on the speckless green.

HOBBLED

He envisaged, poor runaway,
his feet stepping lightly beyond
slave-holding, dead-end Tennessee;
beyond toiling fields, raw dirt roads
       towards, Lord, a promised land.

And not the knife which would requite;
nor being set back in old haunts;
nor the distinctive, limping gait
that would imprint the dust, would bear
       the traces of his faring.

DARTS

The bedroom where his corpse was found
had a bachelor air: strewn clothes;
a cracked mug filling with fag butts;
the chewed biro in the middle
of a crossword puzzle. No note:

as if nothing needed saying.
But where he used to practise darts,
off-the-target throws pricked the door:
swarming – so an old man put it –
like midges around the board.

EFFECTS

When they fished him from the river,
this young man in oil-stained overalls,
we couldn't but recall him

filling petrol, mending punctures:
quiet and obliging behind
the dark stubble, pebble glasses...

Until, examining
his personal effects, they found,
amid an unsuspected hoard

of sketches, one finished painting.
Which left me wondering:
was it omen or *cri-de-coeur*,

this garish piece, this finger-splaying
hand rising out of water
unreally blue and rippleless?

GRAVESIDE

Summer, meadow-scent.
And this burial
in Errill.

After the solemn words,
the press of flesh,
the tolling bells,

memories of him —
The step-perfecting dancer.
His farmer's hands. Yarns snagging

on his smoker's cough.
The boyish features paling
as he pined away —

already shrivelling
as clay thuds
on the coffin lid...

Until his widow
breaks through the barely
alleviating

rituals, bawling
Johnny, Johnny
as if nothing —

HERE

Here, even shops still opening
to the latest news, just-in stock;
even cars revving up the dawn
are going down ancient tracks.

Each blade of grass is spoken for,
each patch of bog and right of way.
That overgrown lane, they'll tell you,
was a Mass path in the Penal days.

These hi-tech farms sprouted from hoed drills,
straining horses, pits, ricks and roosts.
Behind modcon rooms pulse scrub-rough
hands, loosening corsets: palimpsests!

Here, unwittingly, players raise
their forefathers' duds and aces;
those wobbling now towards closing time
are draining ghostly glasses.

AFTER

A rash of premises
and houses for sale or rent.

Behind padlocked entrances,
barren interiors,

sagged Venetian blinds
and fireless grates...

History chronicled in paint,
layer by peeling layer:

navy, aquamarine,
bottlegreen, bare.

*

A deserted creperie
proclaims *Oh La La!*

in bright red letters.
Sounds rise from school playgrounds.

Bets are laid. Women
riffle through bargain rails.

*

The last regulars raise
glasses for refilling:

detonating shorts,
effervescent beers,

slowly-settling Guinness.
The dream-quickening gulps

turning, before their eyes,
to froth, clinging residues.

*

The signposts poised like wings:
Ennis Galway Shannon

Boston Melbourne El Dorado...

SPECTRAL

Even still, the coin which sends
the pool balls tumbling
down that worn chute

would sometimes resurrect
Little Paddy. Absolved,
miraculously,

of his smoker's wheeze,
the twitchy shots, his late
fumbling for the keys,

he'd stand there again,
in hush suspended,
steering the white, god-like,

through scattered colours;
sinking the black
with an impish flourish...

Until he'd slip beyond
our fond words, beyond the call
of *Closing time!*;

and the frothy swish
of rinsing glasses
clinking in our ears.

ADVENT

Outside the church, a few cars:
the still faithful souls keeping vigil.

Down the streets, lights on, houses closed
against the glooming afternoon.

Relic-like, pushing her bicycle,
a stooped, headscarfed woman.

That pasty-faced bachelor straggling
homewards in his steadfast anorak.

At pub doors, eyes hazy, poised
between somewhere and somewhere else...

Yet, even here, who knows
what bone china is tinkling

in memory's parlour,
what muted smithereens?

FAITH HEALER

So one night, years after, she resurfaced,
randomly, in talk. Whoever bought her house,
    Joe Mahon said, just knocked it down;

rebuilding on the site. Would that not bring
bad luck, like interfering with a rath?
    And what happened to her relics?

Ger Breen recalled a clerical student
who came, mere days from ordination, his hands
    red-raw with rash. She healed him, but

could take no recompense. How used she cope?
they wondered. Her every need was sacrificed
    to that austere, God-given gift.

Jim Cleere remembered her curing Burke's shingles.
Although it was winter, she had to quench
    the fire, and kindle it anew.

When this was lighting, she took out a coal;
and shook water on it, chanting chanting:
    Water kills fire! Water kills fire!

Then, having applied the relics, she sprinkled
the cold water on his afflicted flesh —
    how those drops evaporated!

And I, too, thought of her: drab-aproned, gaunt;
there, treating me, a child with scabby sores.
    I squirmed in her piercing eyes...

Eventually, she gave up the healing,
complaining that she could no longer bear
    the rigours of prayer and fasting.

She grew even odder, more reclusive:
suspecting, for instance, that a stranger,
   sighted locally, intended

to break into her home; or that begging
tinker women meant to steal the relics…
   As if, Mahon speculated,

the toll of healing had somehow warped the gift:
as her being dribbled away, behind
   the locked doors, the firmly drawn blinds.

REPORT

When my father read from the local paper
that the grumpy, often tipsy man, who'd come
in a battered van selling calves, had been killed
(accidentally, they said) while shooting game –
his gun discharging as he crossed a stile –
I was barely ten. And I took it all in...

Today, it could be a different story.
I beat memory's path – but what can I flush
out of that November fog? Not pheasants
rising, nor bags filling; nor stubbles bristling
against his muddy boots. Nothing only
the gun: its tantalising, stark report.

BLIGHT

These humid days would have roused my father,
that history-riddled man, out of his rut:
leaning his ear into the fuzzy wireless
    for warnings of potato blight.

I would help him ready the barrel sprayer;
pump the water for the bluestone brew,
stir in the lime and copper sulphate till
    I knew by heart the formula.

In time, I, too, learnt the danger signs.
Days which felt clammy, yet moist and overcast.
Spore-bearing winds. Evenings dense with midges.
    Wet foliage. A sticky mist.

Yet, for all my fervour, I'd keep stumbling
on symptoms: leaves and stems a blotching brown;
undersides a doom-coated down; tuber rot,
    chestnut-hued beneath the skin.

Torn between fascination and dismay,
I'd rush to tell him. *Go away!* he'd shout.
*The badness breaking out...*Then, his ghostly,
    peeved rebuke: *Too late, too late.*

GARDENER

After breaking new ground —
my father's son, at last! —

I find, not shoots pushing up
to burgeon in unthinned green,

but days of pitiless sun,
desiccating winds;

the potato stalks wilting,
scallions tipped with yellow.

And I there, between furrows,
with a dribbly watering can.

Day after day, scanning the sky:
waiting, praying for rain.

HAY

The meadows I have known,
those swaths I used to turn

with a rhythmic nudge of prongs
to be mellowed by breeze and sun,

now quiver in the teeth of blades,
seep out of silage pits.

VISITATION

I was woken, in the small hours,
out of a vaguely troubled sleep.

Hearing persistent sounds — as if
forebodings had been made real —

I found cattle trampling the lawn:
my precious green violated...

Eventually, bringing bales
of hay, Doyle arrived; wondering

what stray had come upon his herd.
Watching him saunter there, I thought,

dartingly, of what might have been;
as the hungry cattle, sniffing hay,

trailed him back through the scanty grass,
through the boundaries they had broken.

DEATHBED

Emerging from
the ICU – after
the vigils, the prayers,

the slipping out of
consciousness – still clinging
to vestiges of Jim

(his quips rippling
through a gathering;
the discreet kindnesses;

his resilience
as cancer ravaged),
I shed the protective

plastic bib; impul-
sively squeezing it
to a fist-sized ball

that was swallowed
in the jaw-snapping
waste disposal bin.

HARVESTING

The evenings shrinking.
Shrouding fogs. Birds brooding
on the power lines...

Is this where I am?
My pen merely a rake
tending these shedding leaves?

*

Here, amid the reaping
and gathering and filling barns,

mute, ubiquitous
blightings, might-have-beens.

On bumpy roads, sods of turf
jolted off homebound loads.

Blemished bales shunted
away to rot in ditches.

Those windfalls, their russet hue
bruised to tainting brown.

*

Stubble fields. Deepening ruts.

But still this yearning to rise
through words and rhythms,

to set a poem flowing.
I'm a pipe fit to burst:

against the old dismay —
Mop it up! Call a plumber! —

secretly exulting
in the gush and spillage.

*

Our bed made for barer nights,
I still wait, bowstring-taut,

for your yielding embrace,
that leaf-quivering release.

BLACK ICE

It came back to me the other day,
those wintry spells I'd known as a boy:
the fern-patterned windows; whitened grass;
the airy sway and carry as I slid
on Ryan's pond or down the road.

But this was different. A sudden wobble,
going to work: black ice, invisible,
stealthy. Against all experience –
my judgment numbed – I panicked, braked.
The car veered: I felt helpless, shaken.

Oh, it was a jolt, nothing much,
no danger of sinking in a ditch.
Nothing much... Only the lingering sense
of journeys still fraught with randomness
and fret, the treachery of ice.

WEDDINGS

Sometimes, looking back,
it all seems like the *Afters*
of a wedding...

To sense you've come too late,
the best already over:
the church ceremony,

its blessings and exchange
of vows; the photo-record;
the meal itself.

To find drink flowing,
and the loosened tongues
renewing ties & feel

you are merely straining
to be absorbed into
what's gone beyond you.

Then, before you know it
almost, the bride and groom
are going away;

and the wedding
is receding
from your waving hand.

DIVINING

When I cast for that altar now —
the bread, the wine; the bowed heads; up-
      lifting *Introibo* —

what stirs is not some hoary god;
but words quickening, binding until
      I'm shaking like a rod.

SKIP

i.m. JK

For weeks afterwards,
whenever I passed by,
I'd note your final washing
left hanging out to dry.

There, too, a mattress slung
over the side of a skip;
its stains outlined, jagged.
Inkblots. Islands. A map...

I'd think of you groping
for bearings down that word-mine;
yet never coming up
with reconciling lines.

I'd think of how you'd shelter
strays; the mock priestly black
you wore; the booze-charged voice:
We poets are unique!

Or how, behind frayed curtains,
the peeling yellow door,
they'd found your body cold,
fallen down the stairs...

And even when the skip
was gone, I could see it still:
dented, the lettering
gappy... Unfillable.

PASSWORDS

i.m. Dennis O'Driscoll

We were visiting relatives;
greeting cousins at midnight Mass:
Yiz are welcome! Roots. Renewals.
Christmas fare in house after house…

When the news – garbled, strange – was brought:
Coll – Cull? …Thurles… illness… poet.
Leaving me to pick up the pieces.
But, before I could well say it,

I thought I glimpsed him, one last time,
knocking at the closed winter inns;
trying every door until
he found the words to let him in.

FLUTTERS

That bachelor uncle I knew
merely from scraps heard as a child.
Tinkering, they'd say, with tractors,
while crops and cattle went astray.
    Lingering at fairs.

A hail-fellow-well-met, they sighed.
Reeling home at all hours from cards
or the races. Until he died,
prematurely, of heart disease.
    But, sometimes, deep in words,

I sense him flickering, hovering.
He's shuffling, dealing out the hands;
or shouting as hooves quicken towards the line...
Then blurs to flutters, resolving
    odds. Aces. Also-rans.

AFTERTHOUGHTS

Boundary Hedge

Father, when you took a notion
to trim down the boundary hedge
between the parent home and mine,
I could hardly contain my rage

at how you'd marred that whitethorn screen.
You, of course, would not waver.
But now, long after you have gone,
it's still there, as strong as ever.

Slip Knots

In a springcleaning burst, I try
to clear the old freezer. Lifting
the lid, I find ice, ice: even
plastic wraps feel stiff and brittling;

the bags you tied are hard as stones.
Gooseberries. Carrots. Peas. Sliced pans.
Your relished side of bacon. Fish
kept for Fridays. A clutch of buns...

Still, after all we had been through,
I'd slip these knots, if I could tell
what yet would thaw to savouring
from what's no longer edible.

GERMINAL

The diaries you kept, mother,
like a fenced-off paddock,
did my pen somehow

emerge from those?
Each day's allotted
space as confining

as your corset or apron:
only leaving room
for barely recorded

births, marriages and deaths;
church-going; your children's
ailments; the fickle weather...

Dutiful, decorous,
yet never expressing
the essential you:

your playful flashes;
your broody, fretted depths;
your airy reaches;

the animated eye
for character and foible.
Did my pen emerge from that?

And was I to be the bull,
snorting at the gate, bursting
through your hedges?

MINING

It still goes on, this des-
cending into inky darkness.
  And we still go on, dearest,

  even as you fret through
my emerging, blackened, racked with
  coughing, wheezy breathing;

  even as I keep faith
with opened seams and yielding layers,
  tongues of fire for winter.

SPECULATING

But (you sometimes counter)
if they violated

every hallowed well;
uprooted every hedge;

and buried the yielding greens
under concrete, under toxins,

wouldn't you still be there,
versifying

upon the mute remains?

THINNING

Do you recall, my love,
the thinning fields we summered in?

And how we'd pluck the scraws
to let our chosen plants develop?..

So, when you take me now,
cherish these clinging roots, cherish

the ground which moulds and nourishes.
If you shook off this clay,

I would wither in your furrows.

LIGHT THE FIRE

Now, when we merely flick a switch,
heat stirs the rads, courses

through the arteries of the house,
exactly as we would wish...

Yet something in me still
yearns for the making of a fire.

To face that monkish cold.
To risk the sting of smoke blown back.

To wait, tense, for wobbly
tongues to take, quicken into blaze.

To sift for glowing coals
in the ashes of the real.

NOCTURNAL

Down in the village,
church and cemetery
keep silent vigil.

Cars are congregated
outside pubs, and the neon-
lit takeaway...

Out here, on the edge
of calculated farms,
newfangled bungalows;

amid weathered signposts
and uneven roads,
you and I blur

to climax: need
raising us fleetingly
beyond ourselves,

and the set seed.

PATRICK MORAN was born in Templetuohy, County Tipperary, where he still lives with his wife and family. He is a retired post-primary teacher. He has won the Gerard Manley Hopkins Poetry Prize; he has also been a winner at Listowel Writers' Week. In 1990, he was shortlisted for the Hennessy/Sunday Tribune Poetry Award. His poem, "Bulbs", won Poem for The Ploughing at the 2015 Ploughing Championships. His work is featured in anthologies, including the inaugural *Forward Book of Poetry* (UK), *The Stony Thursday Book*, as well as *The Best of Irish Poetry 2007* and *Best Irish Poetry 2010*. He is also represented in the recently published *Windharp: Poems of Ireland Since 1916*. His work has been broadcast on the RTE radio programme, *Sunday Miscellany*. His previous collections of poetry are *The Stubble Fields* (Dedalus Press, 2001) and *Green* (Salmon Poetry, 2008).